PASSPORT
TO A SUCCESSFUL LIFE OVERSEAS

8 UNSPOKEN RULES AND ETIQUETTE NO ONE DISCUSSES WITH NRIS

PARAS KUMAR
HELPING INDIANS ABROAD

Copyright © 2025

Paras Kumar

All rights reserved. You may not copy, store, distribute, transmit, reproduce or otherwise make available this publication (or any part of it) in any form, or by any means (electronic, digital, optical, mechanical, photocopying, recording or otherwise), without the prior written permission of the publisher. Any person who does any unauthorised act in relation to this publication may be liable to criminal prosecution and civil claims for damages.

ISBN: 978-1-7638822-1-8

www.parasperspective.com

Dedication

I dedicate this book to all of my friends, my overseas friends, my parents, my sister, and my family friends. You have always supported me in my decisions—even the ones that seemed a bit crazy at times. Your unwavering belief in me has meant the world, and for that, I am forever grateful.

A special acknowledgment goes to my life experiences—both the highs and the lows, the successes and the failures. Each one has been a teacher. While I cherish the good times, it's the difficult moments and failures that have shaped me the most. In those times, I've always asked myself: What is this failure teaching me? What lesson can I learn from this? And I've made it a point to promise myself not to repeat the same mistake again—because the same actions will always lead to the same results.

This book is a collection of my firsthand experiences—both the good and the bad. I hope you enjoy reading it as much as I've valued living and learning through them.

Table of Contents

Introduction 1

Chapter 1 : The Realities of Living Abroad 5

    Living Abroad: Facts and Myths 7

    Culture Shock: Understanding and Adapting 9

    Adapting Strategies 13

    Homesickness and Loneliness: Strategies to Combat ... 15

    Tools For Building Resilience 19

Chapter 2 - Public Etiquette and Public Transport Etiquette 23

    Public Etiquette 25

    Public Transport Etiquette 33

Chapter 3 - Handling Communication and Accent-Related Issues 41

    The Importance of Clear Communication Abroad 42

    Why Do Indians Change Their Accents Abroad? 48

    Mastering Communication Abroad 49

Chapter 4: Mastering Office Etiquette Abroad 53

    Office Etiquette 57

Top Tips for Advancing Your Career Abroad 69

Chapter 5: Dealing With Racism And Stereotype 77

    Racism Exists – The Harsh Reality.................................. 79

    Understanding The Mindset Behind Racism 81

    Coping with Racism: Tips and Strategies 83

Chapter 6- Coping With Loneliness Abroad - Socialising And Making Friends Overseas 93

    Loneliness When Living Abroad 94

    Coping With Loneliness - How to Make Friends and Socialise Abroad 100

    Socialising Rules 106

Chapter 7 Dating And Relationships Abroad 109

    Dreams Versus Marriage 110

    The Rising Indian Divorces - What's Going On? 117

    Important Dating Tips - Dos and Don'ts 123

Chapter 8 Fitness Tips and Gym Etiquette Abroad 133

    You Can Be Fit and Build Muscle Even in Your 30s and 40s 135

    Tips for Maintaining Long-Term Fitness 142

What Type of Exercise is Best Suited For You?...........145

Injuries in the 30s and 40s And Tips to Avoid Them 149

Gym Etiquette - Dos and Don'ts 152

Epilogue – A Story of Growth 159

Conclusion - 8 Lessons for a Successful Life Abroad for NRIs 169

Introduction

When you prepared for overseas education, did your coaching institute offer any guidance on managing homesickness or loneliness? Similarly, as a professional heading abroad for work, were you provided with training to navigate the challenges of living and working in a foreign country?

I certainly didn't. When my company first sent me to the UK and later to South Africa, I had to navigate everything myself. Most companies provide a basic HR orientation covering practicalities such as getting a bus pass, budgeting, and finding affordable groceries. However, they rarely address the aspects that truly impact the quality of life—dealing with racism, adhering to workplace etiquette, dressing smartly, or practising proper table manners.

From understanding cultural nuances to coping with loneliness at weekends and overcoming culture shock, I had to learn everything through trial and error. That's what inspired me to put together this guide, as the things I went through were valuable lessons I wanted to share.

Living abroad can be an extraordinary journey, offering a better quality of life, unparalleled career growth, and opportunities to broaden your horizons. But what about the weekends when the novelty wears off and the realities of being far from home sink in? What about the subtle differences in workplace culture or the unspoken rules of social etiquette? Navigating these challenges without proper preparation can feel overwhelming.

This book is a practical guide designed to help Indians succeed abroad while maintaining their unique identity.

Whether you're an expat, a student, or a professional starting a new chapter in a foreign land, this book aims to equip you with the tools to represent India with pride on the global stage.

Through a mix of real-life case studies and actionable examples, we'll explore the opportunities and hurdles of living abroad. You'll learn how to build meaningful connections, adapt to different environments, and navigate tricky situations with confidence.

Living in a foreign country is not just about survival; it's about thriving. This guide provides the insights and strategies to make your experience abroad fulfilling, rewarding, and truly unforgettable.

You won't find this training in any IELTS coaching centre, migration agents, or company training!

Read on to understand how we can become proud ambassadors of India!

Chapter 1

The Realities of Living Abroad - What No One Tells You

When I first heard that I was being sent to the UK for an onsite opportunity, I was overwhelmed with excitement. It had only been six months since I started my job in a top MNC in Gurgaon, and here I was, about to embark on an international journey.

Although I had travelled abroad as a tourist before, having never been abroad for work, my mind raced with images of picturesque landscapes, professional growth, and a new life of independence. My company provided basic training on where to shop and how to live frugally, but nothing could have prepared me for the reality that awaited. Living abroad and visiting that country as a tourist are very different things. Sharing a flat with two strangers, navigating cultural differences, and battling waves of loneliness and homesickness were just some of the challenges I faced. Even public etiquette on trains and public transport starkly contrasted with how we travelled back home.

In this chapter, I hope to shed light on these realities and offer guidance to fellow Indians who aspire to live and thrive abroad. Read on to discover practical lessons and strategies to make your journey smoother.

Living Abroad: Facts and Myths

As mentioned earlier, living and working in a country is a completely different experience from simply visiting it as a tourist.

What People Imagine

For many, living abroad is synonymous with a glamorous lifestyle, financial stability, and personal freedom. Social media amplifies this perception with photos of scenic vacations, modern apartments, and seemingly effortless success. Friends and family often view your move as a grand achievement and expect glowing updates.

The Reality

The truth, however, is more complex. Adjusting to life abroad involves a steep learning curve, especially when dealing with mundane yet critical tasks like managing bills, navigating public transport, or grocery shopping. High living costs often mean sharing accommodation, sometimes with people from entirely different cultures or lifestyles.

Daily life can feel isolating, particularly if you don't have a support network in place.

Culture Shock: Understanding and Adapting to Different Cultural Norms

Initial Impressions

Despite globalisation, many norms might feel alien when you first start living and working abroad.

When I arrived in the UK, I lived with flatmates who helped me adjust. They guided me in buying clothes—affordable and suitable for the local culture. With fewer responsibilities (I was just 25 years old!), I focused on building a decent wardrobe, including ties for work.

At work, most communication was via audio calls, showing only our faces. My onsite manager, Lorna, and Rajneesh, an Indian manager in the UK for years, were often on these calls. Everyone addressed each other formally as "Sir" or "Ma'am."

Here's a photo of what I wore:

2011 - First job in UK office.

We got basic soft-skills training, but no one guided us on cultural behaviour. Practical advice was limited to keeping the office kitchen clean. Clothing differences stood out—the Brits wore better quality and style compared to Indians. Indians who had travelled from India for an on-site project were easy to spot. In contrast, the British Indians dressed as impeccably as the locals, blending seamlessly into the crowd. It was evident who had come from India and who was born and raised in the UK.

My style was balanced but still made me stand out as an Indian.

The British accent was another challenge—heavy and hard to understand. While some avoided talking to Indians, I pushed through and adapted. I deliberately chose to live with three non-Indians so I'd be forced to learn English. My English evolved, picking up a local touch, which made my Indian friends tease me for "turning firangi." But I saw it as blending in.

2011: My UK friends

Indians are often direct—straight to work, no small talk. In India, managers reprimanded us for tardiness stating that our billing would be affected. In the UK, clients were relaxed, never scolding or penalising us. You could say that this was a positive culture shock—first-name basis, no "Sir" or "Ma'am," and a more laid-back vibe. At the same time, they were extremely disciplined and punctual. A meeting supposed to start at 9 a.m. meant they would be there at 9 a.m. sharp. Not 9:10 a.m.!

Food was another shock—moving from familiar Indian flavours to an international palate was a big change. This was no longer just interstate diversity but a global adjustment.

Let us talk about strategies to use so you can adapt better to culture shock:

Adapting Strategies

- **Observation and Patience**:
  Pay attention to how locals behave and adapt accordingly. Simple acts like saying "thank you" and

"please" or queuing for services reflect cultural respect.

- **Ask Questions:**
Don't hesitate to ask colleagues or friends about cultural nuances. Most people appreciate genuine curiosity.

2016: Boxing class in Sydney

- **Participate in Local Events:**
  Don't stick to your own little group of *desis*. Community gatherings, cultural festivals, and workplace events/parties are excellent opportunities to integrate.

Homesickness and Loneliness: Strategies to Combat These Feelings

The Emotional Toll

After work, we often went out for drinks, a common practice in the UK. (I will delve into this further in the office etiquette chapter). Weekends, however, posed a different dynamic.

In India, weekends meant carefree outings, lively gatherings, or vibrant parties with friends and family—things that didn't require much planning. But abroad, weekends came with responsibilities: buying groceries, cleaning the house, and doing laundry would take up our time. These were tasks many Indian boys, myself included, hadn't typically handled before.

Despite this, we found our rhythm. Saturday evenings became our time to unwind, often stepping out to explore the city. Sundays, on the other hand, were for relaxation. We'd spend hours on Skype or Yahoo Messenger, catching up with friends back home, adjusting for the time difference. Yet, I couldn't shake the pang of homesickness when hearing about the cricket matches we used to play and I couldn't join anymore.

The UK, with its gloomy weather and quiet streets, added to the sense of isolation. Unlike the bustling life I was used to in India, there were days I didn't see another soul, and the loneliness weighed heavily on me. It wasn't easy, but I learned to accept the reality. Homesickness and loneliness are parts of the journey, and embracing them is extremely important when adjusting to life abroad.

Here are some practical solutions to tackle this issue:

- **Stay Connected:**
  Regular video calls with family and friends can offer emotional support.

- **Create Familiar Comforts:**
  Learn to cook traditional dishes or join local Indian communities to stay connected with your roots.

- **Explore Hobbies:**
  Engage in activities like photography, fitness, or learning a new skill can fill your free time constructively. You might even make some local or desi friends along the way!

- **Force yourself to get involved even if you don't feel like it** – join meetup groups, explore events happening around on Facebook and never miss any party invite whether it's an office dinner or social gathering.

- **Seek Professional Help:**
  If feelings of loneliness persist, consider reaching out to a counsellor or therapist.

Tools For Building Resilience

Living abroad pushes you out of your comfort zone. Building resilience is key to thriving in this new environment. Here are some tips:

- **Set Realistic Expectations:**
  Understand that challenges are a part of the process. Success doesn't happen overnight.

- **Develop a Routine:**
  A structured day helps bring stability and focus.

- **Cultivate Friendships:**
  Whether through work, hobbies, or social apps, forming connections can ease feelings of isolation.

- **Invest in Self-Care:**
  Regular exercise, mindfulness practices, and maintaining a healthy lifestyle are essential for mental well-being.

Moving abroad is a transformative experience that tests your limits while offering unparalleled growth opportunities. My journey to the UK and later South Africa and Australia taught me invaluable lessons about adaptability, resilience, and the importance of community. For fellow Indians dreaming of a life abroad, I hope this chapter provides a roadmap to navigate the highs and lows.

Challenges will come, but with preparation and a positive mindset, you can turn them into stepping stones for success.

In the next chapter, I discuss public and transport etiquette rules to enhance your global career.

Chapter 2

Public Etiquette and Public Transport Etiquette

Before I purchased my first car in Australia—and even during my time in the UK—I was heavily dependent on public transport. Trains, buses, and the occasional tram were my primary modes of getting around. Let me tell you, navigating public transport abroad is a whole new experience compared to India. Trains are remarkably quiet, buses adhere to strict schedules, and queues are not just a formality—people genuinely respect them!

2024: Light Rail at Town Hall, Sydney

This chapter will explore essential guidelines and soft skills regarding public and transport etiquette in international settings.

Public Etiquette

Navigating public spaces abroad is a world apart from the *"chalta hai"* attitude often seen in India. These spaces demand respect for personal boundaries, cleanliness, and considerate behaviour, which can leave lasting impressions on those around you. Here's how you can adapt:

Empathy and Greeting
Empathy and greetings transcend words—they're about acknowledging the shared humanity in others and fostering connections. When abroad, the act of "meet and greet" becomes particularly important. A simple "Hello" or "Good morning" to a barista or shop assistant isn't just polite; it's often expected in many cultures outside India. This small gesture not only creates a welcoming atmosphere but also reflects your respect for local customs and approachability.

Equally important are polite expressions like "please" when making a request and "thank you" when receiving something. These small acts of courtesy leave a lasting impression and go a long way in building positive interactions.

Volume Control and Language Choice in Public Places

It's common for Indians to speak in their native language or Hindi in groups, even when others in the group or nearby don't understand it. This also happens in public places as well, like during phone conversations, and that too at a loud volume. While it may not be intentional, it can come across as exclusionary and make others feel left out or uncomfortable—some non-Indians might even think you are talking about them! Allow me to provide an example: Imagine you're a Delhiite who has been transferred to your company's Chennai office. How would you feel when everyone around you communicates in Tamil?

In multicultural settings, it's important to use a language everyone understands, typically English, to promote inclusivity. If you need to switch to your mother tongue, keep it brief, lower your volume, and, when in a group, acknowledge why. If needed, explain what you said. These small gestures can make a big difference in ensuring everyone feels respected and included.

Escalator Etiquette

The use of escalators abroad also comes with a set of etiquette rules. Let me explain.

If you are standing on the escalator- not walking- always stay on the left so people in a hurry can easily pass you from the right side.

Every country might be slightly different - for example, in the UK and Australia, you have to stand on the left of the escalator whereas in Europe, it is to your right. Observe what other people do, and follow the same.

Staring In Public

A friend's mother recently visited Australia. We were in a park where an Australian child- aged 8-10 years old- was playing. They had blue eyes and blonde hair- simply angelic! Aunty Ji could not resist staring at the kid. And as if that wasn't enough - she even went over and picked the kid up! She did not mean any harm but the child's mother took offense. She politely asked Auntyji not to touch her kid!

Please, everyone, let's avoid staring when you are abroad—it's not just about boys staring at girls. Even visiting uncles and aunties keep staring at locals—their attire, appearance, or even how they eat. Perhaps it happens subconsciously. After all, we're only accustomed to seeing such strikingly beautiful people on television, and it's natural to be awestruck by their charm.

However, let me tell you this: staring makes people feel extremely uncomfortable. Instead, admire their beauty discreetly or offer a kind compliment if appropriate, but never stare in a way that comes across as rude or invasive. Let's be mindful and respectful in public spaces.

Be Mindful in Public Places

In India, we're used to walking on the left, but in places like Europe and the US, it's the opposite. When Indians first arrive in these countries, they often stick to the left and end up bumping into others. Nowadays, many of us are also glued to our phones, which can lead to collisions or sudden stops, causing inconvenience to those behind us.

Be mindful of your surroundings—stay alert and aware of what's happening around you. Avoid taking up too much space while walking, and try to move with the flow of the crowd. Maintain the pace, don't stop unnecessarily, and adjust to the rhythm of the people around you.

Holding Doors and Queuing

Whether you are in an office building, a mall, or a busy hotel- always check behind you if any other person is coming, before letting the automatic door swing shut. It is very rude if you let the door bang on some other person's face. Hold the door open until they come in. That's good manners.

Of course, use your common sense here. Do not keep holding the door open for any person who is very far away from you…else they might have to run unnecessarily to catch up.

Secondly, queueing up. This is non-negotiable. Whether it's for entering into a theatre or museum - queues are sacred. Your number will come! Don't jump lines or casually sidle up to the front. Once, in Melbourne, I saw a fellow Indian innocently skip the queue. The muttered "Oh, for heaven's sake" from a nearby Aussie said it all. It is plain disrespectful.

Parking Etiquette - Always Park in the Lane

Always park your car properly within the provided space- the tyres should be within the lines- never on or outside the line.

Understand that parking spots are limited. If you happen to keep your car tyres outside the markings, another car won't be able to park. Traffic cops will come and place a parking ticket on your car and you will be penalised.

Public Transport Etiquette

Public transport abroad is often a punctual, orderly experience. However, it's more than just getting from A to B – it's about respecting the system and those sharing the space.

1. **Understand the Local System**
   Familiarise yourself with the transport network before travelling. London, for instance, uses an Oyster card to

tap in and out, while Sydney relies on Opal cards. Missing simple steps like validating your ticket can result in hefty fines.

2. **Follow Queue Etiquette**

   As mentioned above, queues are non-negotiable. So, be a line maker, not a line breaker! Whether boarding a bus, train, or tram, always wait your turn. Skipping the line, even unintentionally, can be perceived as rude.

3. **Respect Personal Space**

   Close encounters are only nice in sci-fi movies- not on public transport abroad! People here treat their personal space as the Laxman Rekha - it is sacred! So give people space. The next time you travel on public transport overseas, remember there is an invisible board around all your fellow passengers saying "This is my limit- do not cross this".

If it's crowded, keep your movements subtle and avoid bumping into others. A small nod or "sorry" goes a long way if you accidentally do.

4. **Mind Your Volume**

   As stated earlier, do not speak loudly in your language when riding the bus or train. Take the call, but keep your volume down.

   Please use headphones for music or videos, ensuring the volume is low. Avoid noisy snacks or talking loudly during short rides, as this can disturb others.

5. **Maintain Personal Hygiene**

   Body odour? Big no. Smelling like yesterday's curry? Even bigger no. Invest in a good deodorant and wear clean clothes. If your apartment smells of curry, your clothes might carry that smell. So, air it out from time to time - especially after cooking!

6. **Don't Look into Your Fellow Travellers' Phones**

   Yes - curiosity often leads us to glance at someone else's phone screen in public. But this behaviour is often considered intrusive and impolite. It is important to respect the personal boundaries of others, especially when travelling or living abroad.

   Instead, focus on your activities, and avoid appearing to pry into what others are doing on their devices. Practising such discretion will not only make you appear courteous but will also help you blend seamlessly into cultures where personal privacy is regarded as a social norm.

7. **Don't Point Fingers at People**

   Pointing fingers directly at someone is often perceived as rude or confrontational in many cultures. While it might be a casual or instinctive gesture in some parts of India, in Western countries and other international settings, it can come across as accusatory or disrespectful.

Instead, if you need to gesture towards someone, use an open hand or a subtle nod. This conveys your intention in a polite and non-threatening manner. Adopting this small but significant change in body language demonstrates cultural sensitivity and respect for those around you.

8. **Don't Scratch Your Crotch Publicly**

   This action is considered highly inappropriate and unhygienic in most cultures. Such behaviour can make your fellow travellers uncomfortable and is often seen as a breach of basic social etiquette. If possible, move to the toilet or washroom and address the itch discreetly.

9. **Mind Your Eating Habits**

   While Indian curries and dishes are undeniably delicious, their strong aromas may not be welcome in confined spaces like buses or trains, where air is recirculated rather than refreshed. Similarly, noisy foods, like crunchy snacks or slurp-heavy meals, can attract unwanted attention.

If you need to eat while travelling, opt for light, odour-free snacks. Being mindful of others' comfort ensures a more pleasant experience for everyone on board.

10. **Acknowledge Drivers**

    A simple "thank you" to bus or tram drivers as you disembark shows gratitude and leaves a positive impression.

    By embracing these public and transport etiquette tips, you'll not only navigate foreign spaces with ease but also reflect the best of Indian culture.

Respect, cleanliness, and courtesy aren't just local customs – they're universal values.

In the next chapter, I will discuss important communication and accent-related tips for Indians studying or working abroad.

Chapter 3

Handling Communication and Accent-Related Issues

Let's do a quick activity: try pronouncing the words "plumber" and "mortgage" in your mind.

No cheating! Now, check their correct pronunciation on Google.

Yes, the "B" is silent [1] in "plumber," and the "T" is not pronounced [2] in "mortgage." If you got that right, give yourself a pat on the back! You already have a solid grasp of English and are less likely to face significant communication challenges abroad.

If not, don't worry—there's a slight learning curve ahead. This chapter focuses on communication skills when living abroad, a crucial area where many Indians face difficulties.

The Importance of Clear Communication Abroad

Clear communication is essential for success abroad, and accent plays a significant role in this. Indians often encounter challenges stemming from their thick accents and unique English pronunciations.

References:
1. How to pronounce Plumber: https://youtu.be/KBgt2-BuNl8
2. How to pronounce Mortgage: https://youtu.be/ilx9eMzVMZU

The Struggles of Non-Native Speakers

Firstly, don't blame yourself if you find communication tricky in a foreign country. After all, we are non-native speakers. Most of us learn English at vernacular schools or from television, and let's face it—English is a peculiar language.

Even Shashi Tharoor, a renowned wordsmith, has highlighted its quirks. Did you know there are seven different pronunciations for words containing the letters "ough"?

Shashi Tharoor

Consider these examples: though, bough, through, thought, cough, enough, hiccough. The variations range from "oh" and "ow" to "oo" and "uff." Mind-boggling, isn't it?

Despite these complexities, it's vital to communicate clearly by adapting to local dialects and accents as necessary.

My Experience

When I first moved to the UK, interacting with colleagues with British accents was a challenge. I often had to ask them to repeat themselves, and they did the same with me. While I managed better than many fellow Indians, some struggled significantly due to poor communication skills.

One of the key criteria for being sent onsite is having strong communication skills. To improve, I deliberately chose to live with non-Indians so I'd be forced to communicate in English. My flatmates were from diverse backgrounds—Chinese, Irish, and others—and their English was often weaker than mine. This taught me an important lesson: if non-native speakers struggled to understand me, native English speakers likely found it even harder.

2016: With Sydney Friends

The Irish accent, in particular, was quite strong, but I noticed an interesting phenomenon. When you interact with people who have different accents, your subconscious mind automatically adjusts your speech. Without realising it, you begin to modify your accent and pronunciation to be better understood.

Later, when I moved to Australia and lived with Europeans, Brazilians, and French flatmates, I again found myself adapting. Despite my initial confidence in my English (which was a lot better than some of the South Americans), I realised the goal wasn't about being "better" than others—it was about ensuring mutual understanding.

Over time, I consciously and subconsciously began adjusting my speech, rolling my "R's" and tweaking my accent to communicate effectively. Fast forward to today: after living in the UK, South Africa, and now Australia, my accent has become a blend—a khichadi of influences I've picked up along the way.

Facing Criticism

This adjustment hasn't come without its drawbacks. I've often been trolled for my accent, with comments like, "Stop faking that accent—it's so artificial and irritating." But this experience isn't unique to me; even top CEOs like Sundar Pichai and Satya Nadella face similar criticism for their accents. They have mixed accents - Indian and American - but they both speak so clearly and fluently that anyone in the world can understand them no matter what their accent/nationality.

Sundar Pichai (CEO of Google) and Satya Nadella (CEO of Microsoft)

Why Do Indians Change Their Accents Abroad?

The answer is simple: to be understood. When I first started working with my British colleagues, their frequent interruptions— "Beg your pardon?" or "Sorry, could you repeat that?"—made it clear that my thick Indian accent was hard to follow.

Repeating myself multiple times became frustrating and embarrassing, so I decided to take matters into my own hands and learn to adapt. Effective communication is about being understood, and many back in India don't fully appreciate this struggle.

When I visited India and inadvertently rolled my "R's," people would laugh, accusing me of trying to act like a *firang* to seem cool. *"Kya style marta hai!"* they'd tease.

Whenever you move to a new country, there's an unspoken expectation to blend into the local culture, including how you speak. It's not superficial—it's about survival and belonging.

Mastering Communication Abroad

Now that we've explored why Indians adapt their accents, let's look at how to overcome these challenges. The key lies in mastering communication.

Learn by Listening

Take inspiration from children born to Indian parents abroad. They naturally pick up local accents because they're surrounded by those phonics, words, and sounds. It does not matter that their parents still communicate with heavy Indian-English accents. Immersion in a language environment makes adaptation almost automatic.

Visiting India with Your "Foreign" Accent

When I visit India, I'm often teased for my accent with comments like, *"Oh, you've become a firang,"* or *"Kitna style maar raha hai."* These remarks stem from a lack of understanding of the pressures and struggles we face abroad.

Handling Criticism

In India, I switch to Hindi (since I am a Delhiite and my mother tongue is Hindi) with friends and family to avoid misunderstandings. For English conversations, I speak slowly and clearly, ensuring I'm understood without overemphasising my accent. If people still criticise, I ask them:

- Was I clear?
- Did you understand me?
- Was my grammar correct?

If the answer is "yes," then I have no reason to worry. Ultimately, effective communication is about clarity and understanding.

If you are going to India for a short visit, I'd strongly recommend sticking to your native/local language at least with friends and family to avoid being judged unnecessarily.

Choose Peace

In general- avoid engaging with negativity and trolls and focus on being authentic. Whether your accent is "Indian" or "foreign," stay true to yourself. Speak slowly, clearly, and confidently—your accent will become irrelevant.

In the next chapter, we'll delve into essential office etiquette rules for thriving abroad.

Chapter 4:

Mastering Office Etiquette Abroad

In many workplaces abroad, Fridays are all about socialising rather than work. Some offices have bars on-site, while others arrange trips to local pubs. It's the perfect chance to bond with colleagues, share funny stories (or work issues), and maybe smooth over any awkward misunderstandings.

2013 - Team in South Africa

When I was at Zensar Technologies, I had the chance to work in South Africa with Discovery Insurance, one of our top clients. To my surprise (and delight), their office bar was well-stocked with beer and whiskey for informal gatherings. It was a great way to network and relax.

Sadly, a few of my Indian colleagues took things way too far. What started as a casual drink turned into something embarrassing. They didn't stop at a few drinks—some drank until they were out of control, pocketed unopened bottles, and even packed snacks and food to take home for the weekend!

The management, of course, noticed. The consequences were swift and embarrassing: a strict ban on all Zensar employees using the bar. Yes, the whole team was blacklisted. Every time we passed that once-welcoming space, it was a walk of shame.

This incident is a good reminder: your technical skills might get you the job, but it's your soft skills—like good workplace etiquette—that help you keep it. When working abroad, you're not just representing yourself—you're also representing your country.

In this chapter, we'll look at two key areas: mastering office etiquette and, the exciting part, top tips to boost your career overseas. Stay tuned—it could make a big difference to your success!

Office Etiquette

Don't Go Overboard with Free Food and Drinks
Never take food or drinks home from office events unless you've been explicitly invited to do so. Such actions are noticed and can leave a lasting negative impression. Sadly, a handful of instances have perpetuated the stereotype of Indians (who are on-site) as freeloaders, and it's embarrassing when the actions of a few tarnishes everyone's reputation. *Kuch logon ki wajah se poore desh ka naam kharab ho jata hain!*

This behaviour is often associated with Indian bachelors, who sometimes overindulge at office gatherings as a way to avoid cooking at home. They pile their plates sky-high at these events, (reminding you of that scene from Three Idiots)—yes, exactly like that!

What many fail to realise is that management, senior bosses, and influential colleagues notice these things. And trust me, it doesn't go unnoticed for the right reasons.

To help you navigate office events without becoming that person, here are three essential rules:

1. **Don't lose your composure over free food**

   Picture this: you've heaped your plate to the brim and are shovelling it down, oblivious to your surroundings. Your focus is entirely on the buffet, with zero effort to engage in conversation, socialise, or network.

   It's not a great look. Balance is key—enjoy the food, but remember that these events are about socialising and building connections.

2. **Observe your colleagues' plates and follow their lead.**

Avoid piling your plate to the point of overflowing on your first go—take modest portions, eat neatly, and if you're still hungry, go for a second helping. This not only reflects good manners but also ensures there's enough for everyone.

3. **Never take food or drinks home unless explicitly invited**

    If the management wants leftovers to be taken home, they'll usually make an announcement or put up a note. Grabbing food uninvited is considered poor etiquette and will only lead to raised eyebrows and quiet whispers.

In short, office events are an opportunity to showcase your professionalism and social skills, not just your appetite. So, keep it classy, and let your good manners be the takeaway—not the food!

Avoid Speaking Loudly in Your Native Language or Hindi

Speaking in your local language or Hindi in office settings, especially when others cannot understand it, is considered rude. Colleagues may feel excluded or suspect that you're discussing something they're not meant to hear. It's far more professional to converse in a language everyone understands.

Refrain from Personal Comments or Questions

Corporate culture overseas is markedly different from what many are accustomed to in India, especially when it comes to personal boundaries. Unless someone is a close friend, avoid making personal remarks about their appearance or mannerisms.

Similarly, refrain from asking intrusive questions about topics such as marital status, sexuality, family, or whether someone has children. For example, questions like *"Are you married?"*, *"What's your sexuality?"*, or *"Why don't you have kids?"* can come across as **insensitive** and **invasive**. Conversations around these topics, particularly sexuality or LGBTQ+ matters, are often private and sensitive, and such questions could inadvertently hurt or alienate your colleagues.

When it comes to appearance, **draw a clear line between compliments and comments**. Remarks like *"You look fat,"* "Your hair is turning grey," or "You look tired with those eye bags," are best avoided unless the individual has already broached the subject or you share a very close bond. Instead, focus on positive, uplifting comments.

Compliments such as *"You look sharp," "You seem very fit,"* or *"That outfit really suits you,"* are generally appreciated and create a pleasant atmosphere without crossing personal boundaries. Remember, kindness and tact go a long way in fostering goodwill in a diverse workplace.

Do Not Discuss Salaries

It is not uncommon for fresh graduates, senior-level professionals new to the corporate world, or newcomers to feel comfortable asking about salaries in casual conversation. However, this is considered **highly inappropriate** and is widely frowned upon in professional settings, particularly in international workplaces.

These discussions are generally seen as intrusive and unprofessional abroad as well as in India. Salary is a personal matter and, in many cultures, is treated as a private topic.

In corporate environments, it's best to steer clear of this subject unless you're discussing compensation with HR or during formal negotiations. Focus instead on building rapport through shared interests or professional discussions that foster goodwill and mutual respect.

Be Mindful During Virtual or Online Meetings

I often find myself wondering—why don't people in India turn on their cameras during virtual meetings? Is it a data-saving strategy?

I now work in an Australian company and am a client of several Indian offshore companies. We also have vendors like Accenture in Bangalore and HCL in Noida. When we conduct online or virtual meetings, I noticed a peculiar trend—the team members almost never switch on their videos. Perhaps they're just camera-shy or saving their internet data for binge-watching movies.

Post-pandemic, virtual or online meetings have become the norm, and with that comes a set of basic etiquette rules to ensure professionalism.

Here are a few tips to keep your virtual meetings smooth and embarrassment-free:

- **Switch on your camera when possible**
  While it's perfectly understandable to keep your camera off on days like a bad hair day, consistently doing so can create the impression of disengagement.

  A visible face fosters connection and engagement, even if it means combing your hair five minutes before the call.

- **Adjust your noise cancellation settings**

    Since I am a client now, I always have virtual meetings with my Indian offshore vendors. It makes me laugh when I hear Indian traffic noise, honking or even vegetable hawkers selling veggies, or that incessant pressure cooker whistle can be distracting and unprofessional. Use noise-cancelling tools or mute your microphone when not speaking to avoid adding unintended chaos to the meeting.

- **Use a green screen/camera background or tidy up your background**

    A plain backdrop or virtual green screen can save you from the embarrassment of someone spotting your clutter or a questionable poster. Remember those viral stories of people unknowingly walking half-naked in the background or babies crawling into the frame during calls? Let's learn from them and avoid becoming the next YouTube sensation.

- **Close unnecessary windows before screen sharing**

  Before hitting "Share Screen," ensure only the relevant tabs are open. No one needs to see your email, especially if it's showcasing details of your next job interview—or worse, your recent Amazon search for embarrassing products.

- **Avoid eating on camera**

  No matter how tempting that plate of samosas looks, munching on camera is unprofessional and distracting. Keep snacks for later, or at least turn off the camera if hunger strikes during the meeting.

Don't Eat at Your Desk

Coming back to our physical office, let's talk about lunchtime office etiquette.

Indian cuisine is renowned for its rich aromas, but the strong and lingering scents can be overwhelming in closed office environments. To ensure a harmonious workplace, always eat your meals in the designated kitchen or cafeteria areas, rather than at your desk.

After your meal, take care to wash your lunchbox in the appropriate facilities and place any used dishes directly into the dishwasher. Avoid leaving dishes unattended or dirty items in the sink, as this can inconvenience colleagues and create an untidy environment. Thoughtful food etiquette helps maintain a pleasant and professional atmosphere for everyone.

Dress Appropriately

Appearances matter in the workplace. Avoid casual T-shirts with loud slogans or oversized trainers. opt for formal attire like shirts and trousers, complemented by polished shoes. Observe your colleagues' dress code and emulate their style to maintain professionalism. If your industry demands it, wear a tie to show your professionalism.

The next section is packed with practical, eye-opening career strategies that will have you saying, *"Why didn't I know this before?"*

These tips aren't just helpful—they're transformative. Follow them, and you'll not only excel professionally but also build a reputation that opens doors to even greater opportunities. You'll surely thank me later for the boost this will give your career!

Top Tips for Advancing Your Career Abroad

The Power of Small Talk: A Key to Workplace Success
Picture this: it's your first day at an overseas job. You step into the office, ready to prove your worth, but as colleagues gather by the coffee machine chatting about last night's game or the unpredictable weather, you quietly settle at your desk. You're hesitant—after all, isn't diving straight into work what productivity is all about?

Here's the thing: small casual talk isn't a distraction; it's a **bridge**. It sets the tone for better workplace relationships and can even shape how colleagues perceive you. In many countries, light conversation is a crucial part of professional culture. While Indian workplaces often prioritise a "straight to business" approach, abroad, a quick chat about local sports, the weather, or trending news isn't just polite—it's expected.

Discussing cricket or the IPL might be your go-to icebreaker in India. Similarly, in Australia, a friendly comment about rugby can work wonders. And let's not forget the ultimate conversation starter—the weather! Everyone has something to say about it, making it the perfect opener.

Engaging in small talk not only builds rapport but also leaves a lasting positive impression. So, don't shy away—embrace those little moments of connection. They could be the key to unlocking bigger opportunities in your career.

Start practising small talk using these icebreakers (sports, weather, or news). You'll notice the difference during your next performance review/appraisal.

Striking the Perfect Balance in Workplace Conversations

In many countries, casual greetings like *"How are you?"* are simply polite gestures, not an open invitation for detailed updates.

I remember my colleague Raj, who would respond with long-winded stories about his personal life. His tales, often bordering on melodrama, left his colleagues visibly uncomfortable. In fact, his anecdotes grew so emotional that one colleague jokingly remarked, *"Bas kar, pagle, rulayega kya!"* ("Stop it, mate, or you'll have us all in tears!").

On the other hand, there was Priya, who swung to the opposite extreme. She was so reserved that she spoke only about work, rarely engaging in casual conversation. She often ate alone and kept to herself, making it challenging for her colleagues to connect with her or build any meaningful rapport.

The key to successful workplace interactions lies in **finding the right balance.** Avoid oversharing personal details, but don't retreat into silence either. Read the room, engage in light and meaningful conversations, and contribute positively to group discussions. This balance helps foster connections, builds trust, and creates a collaborative atmosphere that benefits everyone.

Attend Office Parties and Social Events

If there's one key to accelerating your career, it's office parties. They may seem like a casual break from work, but these gatherings are an invaluable platform for building relationships and advancing your career. Yet, many Indians often skip these events, citing reasons like family responsibilities—picking up kids, cooking dinner, or simply unwinding at home. But here's the truth: it's in these informal settings where the most significant professional connections happen.

2012 - Company event party in UK with colleagues.

Office parties are often where promotions and appraisals are subtly discussed, where you can gain invaluable tips from colleagues, and where your career path can take a positive turn. The casual conversations that unfold over drinks or bowling can offer insights into the company culture, your team's dynamics, and even the next big opportunity.

So, don't miss out. Engage in after-work drinks, team outings, or friendly games—it's all about showing your team spirit and making genuine connections. Remember, those informal chats could be the stepping stone to your next big career move.

Avoid Overindulging at Social Events

Here's a task for you: next time you're at an office party or social event, pay close attention to your bosses. Watch how they mingle, how they position themselves and notice their body language. They may be holding a drink, but don't assume they're indulging. Often, the drink is simply a tool to blend in while they observe how you and your colleagues behave in a relaxed setting. This is a prime opportunity for them to assess your professionalism, social skills, and suitability for future leadership roles. They may even be mentally considering who's ready for promotion.

Now, a crucial tip to remember: avoid over drinking. It's all too easy to let loose in a social setting, but excessive drinking can lead to unprofessional behaviour and even reveal more than you intend.

Maintain composure throughout, reserving celebratory drinking for personal occasions (or with friends or family) where the stakes are lower. Your poise and professionalism in these situations can make a lasting impression on your career.

Embrace Cultural Diversity
Treat colleagues from all backgrounds with respect. Take the opportunity to learn about their cultures, whether Nepali, Sri Lankan, or otherwise. People appreciate genuine curiosity about their traditions, making it a great way to build friendships.

Perfect Your Handshake
A firm handshake is a universal sign of confidence. Stand up when greeting someone who is already standing. Such small gestures speak volumes about your professionalism and respect for others.

By following these guidelines, you'll not only thrive in your career abroad but also enhance India's reputation on the global stage.

In the next chapter, we'll explore how to navigate racism and discrimination when working and living abroad.

Chapter 5:

Dealing with Racism and Stereotype

Have you ever experienced discrimination or racism? I am certain that, at some point, you have. Racism and discrimination are not confined to foreign lands; they exist closer to home as well, even between states within our country.

Remember that iconic scene from Shah Rukh Khan's film *Chak De India*, where the girls from the north-eastern states of India are greeted with, *"Welcome to India!"* She poignantly responds, *"Humare hi desh mein, humko welcome?"*

We all unconsciously discriminate. In many northern Indian states, people harbour biases against those from southern states. Similarly, some South Indians hold prejudices against those who speak Hindi. It's a reality we cannot ignore. We do it subconsciously.

The unfortunate truth is that racism and bias have existed since the beginning of time. Take, for instance, those moments when we are frustrated with our boss and resort to name-calling—whether it's *"fatso"* or *woh sala gora!* These expressions often slip out without thought. Regardless of what laws dictate or rules prescribe, human psychology ensures that racism and bias persist.

In this chapter, I will dive deep into the challenges of facing racism abroad, identify the types of people prone to racist behaviour, and provide strategies to prepare you to handle such situations mentally.

Racism Exists – The Harsh Reality

As I mentioned earlier, judgment, racism, stereotypes, bias, and discrimination have been around since the dawn of time. For instance, we unconsciously treat people from the USA, Europe, or Australia differently than those from Bangladesh, Pakistan, or African nations.

Our behaviour often shifts based on how we answer the question: *"Where are you from?"* Subconsciously, we decide how much respect to extend and how to interact with someone, solely based on this.

Here's another example: Recently, I met a Ukrainian girl who had come to Australia on a protection visa. Almost instinctively, most of us asked about her family and how the Russia-Ukraine war had impacted her. This reaction is common when meeting individuals from war-torn regions like Israel, Iraq, or Syria.

Let me share a personal story. I have a mixed complexion and a strong build, which often makes people think I'm Latino. I matched with a European woman on a dating app, and our conversations started well. After chatting for a while, we decided to meet. My accent is a mix of British, South African, and Australian, which might have kept her from realising I'm Indian. However, when she found out about my Indian background, her attitude changed. She openly said she wouldn't date someone from India.

To this day, I wonder what preconceived notions about Indians led her to make that decision.

I'm not suggesting these experiences are universal or constant. I am merely stating that they happen. Understanding this reality equips you to handle such situations if they arise. In the following sections, I will share tips for navigating discrimination and racism with grace and composure.

Understanding The Mindset Behind Racism

In my experience, it's often individuals from middle-class or lower-middle-class backgrounds who are prone to making stereotypical or racist remarks. Wealthier, more refined individuals, such as millionaires or billionaires, tend to focus on business collaborations or opportunities rather than background or ethnicity.

Unfortunately, the frustration of some middle-class individuals often manifests as resentment, particularly towards Indians, whom they perceive as taking their jobs. These are the people most likely to pass hurtful remarks to destabilise or demoralise you.

To them, I would like to highlight this fact: Indian IT professionals are among the highest taxpayers, significantly contributing to the economies of the countries where they work.

Take Will Smith as an example. Despite being an African-American actor in Hollywood, he rose above potential discrimination to become one of the industry's most successful and admired figures.

His story reminds us that while racism exists, it doesn't have to define or limit us.

Will Smith

Now we will cover the ways to handle racism and bias with poise and grace.

Coping with Racism: Tips and Strategies

1. Build Physical and Mental Strength

Let's be honest: individuals who appear physically strong are less likely to become targets. Someone who perceives you as physically stronger than them is likely to hesitate before making racist remarks, fearing potential consequences. Therefore, prioritise your fitness—eat well, build your strength, and invest in your overall well-being. Strength naturally fosters confidence, and a well-built, resilient appearance can empower you to navigate challenging situations with greater ease and effectiveness.

Beauty Bias and Racism

Let's face an uncomfortable truth: people tend to be more likeable when they are physically attractive and fit. Consider the example of Hrithik Roshan, a Bollywood superstar, and Zach Galifianakis. Be honest—who seems more likable at first glance?

Zach Galifianakis, Actor/Comedian, and Hrithik Roshan, Bollywood Superstar

Now, let's take the example of Aishwarya Rai compared to a female sportsperson from another country.

Aishwarya Rai, Actress

The point here is that a good-looking and well-presented Indian is less likely to encounter racism than someone who appears unkempt or is perceived as unattractive, such as an obese individual from another country. This bias often operates on a subconscious level; people naturally gravitate toward what they find visually appealing. If you are polished, well-dressed, and carry yourself with confidence, you are less likely to become a target of prejudice.

2. **Represent Yourself and Your Country Gracefully**

   Locals can dress as they please, even if that means going barefoot. However, as immigrants, we bear an additional responsibility to represent our home country. It's important, therefore, to ensure we are always presentable and avoid appearing untidy or unkempt. Carry yourself with poise and dignity, avoiding unnecessary conflicts and maintaining a polished and respectful image.

3. **Strive for Success and Wealth**

   Can anyone imagine directing racist comments at Satya Nadella or Sundar Pichai? These visionary CEOs exemplify how success and wealth can transcend racial biases. When you achieve prosperity, people are more likely to view you as a potential partner for business or collaboration rather than as a threat to their rights. **Racist prejudices often take a back seat to ambition and opportunity.**

Focus on excelling in your field, and you are sure to earn a level of **respect** that rises above skin colour or ethnicity.

4. **Prepare Responses for Racist Remarks**

   Racism can occur anywhere—at work, on public transport, in the supermarket or even at family gatherings. Have a few thoughtful, impactful responses ready:

For instance, if someone at work makes a derogatory comment, you might respond, *"As an Indian, I contribute significantly to the economy here. Without Indian IT professionals, many of the systems (trains, etc) your country relies on would fail." "We are the highest taxpayers and we have contributed significantly towards nation-building."*

If you are a student and someone makes racist remarks against you, then remind them that as an international student you are paying four times higher fees than local students which is funding the university.

Think about such answers. Depending on the country you are in, think of a few comebacks with the **angle of the economy** so that the person making the racist remark realises their mistake.

Craft responses that highlight your contribution and make the other person reconsider their prejudice.

5. Avoid Attracting Negative Attention

Refrain from habits such as littering or spitting in public. As stated earlier, you are representing yourself as well as India. So, follow basic rules and etiquette.

When in Rome, do as Romans do. This means you should respect and follow the local customs and culture when staying and working abroad. Dressing in a way that suits the environment and local traditions shows respect and helps you blend in. It can also make things easier and avoid drawing unnecessary attention.

6. Don't Be Overly Sensitive

Sometimes, what appears to be a racist comment may simply be an innocuous joke or remark. It is not always about you- it could be about the environment. Perhaps the guy remarking is just having a bad day. So, learn not to take things so personally. And do toughen up.

Learn to discern intent and avoid overreacting. Develop a sense of humour about yourself to defuse tense situations and create a positive atmosphere.

Laughing at yourself is a powerful way to defuse tension and foster a positive environment. I once had an Italian colleague who would quip, *"I'm Italian; I never come to meetings on time!"* Similarly, when someone at the gym asks about my profession, I often reply with a playful grin, *"Well, I'm Indian, so of course, I'm in IT!"*

By embracing humour and light-heartedness, you can shift the energy of a conversation and create a more relaxed atmosphere. Those around you will often follow your lead and take things less seriously. Conversely, being overly sensitive can draw unnecessary negativity, amplifying the very issues you're trying to avoid.

Do this the next time someone remarks on your punctuality. Jokingly say, *"I'm on Indian Standard Time/IST!"* Such humour will instantly shift the energy of the conversation and prevent the negativity from escalating.

And that concludes my take on facing racism abroad.

In the next chapter, I will share practical tips for socialising and making friends in a foreign land. Stay tuned!

Chapter 6

Coping with Loneliness Abroad - Socialising and Making Friends Overseas

When we relocate abroad, we experience a mix of emotions. On one hand, we are excited about the prospects of a clean pollution-free place with plenty of career growth. On the other hand, we are terrified of leaving behind loved ones—friends and family.

Unfortunately, no one talks about facing loneliness abroad. No one considers this aspect of life in a strange place. The pangs of loneliness, missing loved ones, and hanging out with close friends, on weekends, holidays, and festivals are all very real. And many people go through it.

In this chapter, I will talk about loneliness and how to cope with it when you relocate abroad, tips to socialise and make friends, and some important social etiquette rules to follow when making friends abroad.

Loneliness When Living Abroad

Grab a drink, this topic is heavy.

When you live abroad, come Friday evening, the feeling of loneliness creeps up on you when you get back from the office. The thought of spending the weekend staring at the walls can be daunting.

Sure, you might go out with colleagues for a drink or catch up with some friends or family if you are lucky enough to live close to some. But what about the days, when the weather is bad and you just don't feel like going out? What about the days your friends or relatives are busy with some other plans?

That is when the loneliness hits you.

I feel it the most on days when I come back from the gym and there is no one to cook my protein-rich meals. You have to make your breakfast or if you are getting late, you just grab a coffee and leave for the office. No one calls you to ask, *"Beta, did you eat? Beta, don't forget your lunch!"*

Many Indian bachelors don't like cooking or don't know how to cook- they eat out every day- which makes them miss *ghar ka khana* (home food) even more.

In addition to missing one's family members, you miss your friends. No one calls you on Fridays and weekends. Here, there is an unwritten rule- you cannot call anyone just like that- you need to text and ask them if they are free to talk to you. Unlike in India, you cannot just visit someone here. You need to seek their permission first. In India, you could easily call or visit your childhood friends just like that- no appointment necessary! The best part is they will cheer you up when you are feeling down. Here, you are your own best friend. If you miss your friends back in India, you can call them and reminisce about the good times. But it just does not feel the same as meeting in person.

Then there are **two days** in the year when you feel the lowest- can you guess?

The first day is *Diwali*. I miss my family and friends terribly during this festival. Diwali is so vibrant back home- your friends and family are celebrating and you just wish you could catch the next flight home. Sure, you can call friends and family members or get on video calls but you miss the food, the firecrackers, and the Diwali parties. Here in Australia, even my married friends- despite living with their partners and kids state that they miss the vibe back home- it is just not present in this foreign land.

On Diwali day, I visit the Gurudwara here in Sydney. It feels good to be among other people. But once I come back home in the evening, that loneliness returns.

The second day I feel lonely is my *birthday*. No one is coming at midnight with a cake, no one calls you to wish you. You just go to sleep as you have to go to the office the next day. Sure, you might get some calls from your loved ones from India. But no one will be coming to your doorstep to wish you well. Some friends or family here might invite you on the weekend to celebrate but if your birthday falls on the weekday, then what? People are bound to be busy and they might just wish you but not have the time to visit or take you out.

So, these are the two days, I feel the loneliness.

In India, you have free **therapy** in the form of friends. Here you need to pay a therapist who will listen to you and probably give you some advice or medication! Stress, mental illness, and depression are on the rise here. So therapists are in huge demand here. But do you think they offer the same benefits as a childhood friend? I highly doubt it!

So, loneliness is very much real. And unfortunately, no one talks about it. No one tells you about this aspect of living abroad. Everyone's social media pages may show they are busy- going to the beach, hitting the gym, or driving their posh cars on long drives. But once you are home, behind the scenes, the loneliness comes back to haunt you again.

So, read on to find out how to cope with loneliness and things that help me.

Coping With Loneliness - How to Make Friends and Socialise Abroad

Visiting a country versus actually living there for work are two very different things. Behind those Instagram-worthy photos, the reality is very different. Here are some tips to help you cope with loneliness:

Understand That You Are Not Alone

Understand that there are people who care deeply for you, even from miles away. Maintain virtual connections with your family and friends back in India by scheduling regular daily or weekly calls. If you have loved ones living nearby, take the opportunity to visit them on weekends or invite them to your home. Together, you can enjoy cooking, hiking, or engaging in activities that bring you joy.

Don't Underestimate the Power of Socialising

Step out and explore. Don't stick to making desi friends only. You must avoid staying cooped up at home. Focus on broadening your social circle as doing so can lead to remarkable new experiences with people from diverse backgrounds.

2024 - Hiking with Bondi Outdoors Club at Royal National Park.

Consider joining local clubs and embracing the culture around you. For instance, I recently joined a volleyball club where we play on weekends when the weather permits. It's incredibly enjoyable, and we connect through a shared love for sports and fitness at Bondi Beach. Through this club, I've built meaningful friendships.

Socialising is especially important as loneliness and mental health challenges (anxiety, depression, etc.) can significantly impact your physical well-being and professional growth. Trust me, falling ill while living alone abroad is an experience you want to avoid. Prioritise building connections and engaging with others—it's a vital part of maintaining both mental and physical health.

Embrace Diversity - Be Open Minded

Approach life with an open mind and a flexible attitude. Embrace the richness of local diversity, customs, and cultures. Take the opportunity to learn something new from individuals of different backgrounds. Ask them about their traditions—most people enjoy sharing stories about their culture.

Mindset Matters

This is a pivotal time in your life, and your mind may play tricks on you with questions like, *Did I make the right choice? Have I made a mistake?* Remember, you may never feel completely at home—*ghar ghar hota hai*—and life may seem as though it's taking a U-turn.

It's essential to affirm firmly: Whatever decision I make, it is for the best. Be clear about your career goals—no matter where you go or what path you choose, focus on creating value. Strive not to become a liability to your family, the country you are living in, or the economy. When you commit to adding value, success will follow you wherever you are, and you'll always find your way.

With a positive mindset, the universe will conspire to bring abundance to every aspect of your life.

Find The Right Accommodation

This is an important consideration: who you live with and where you live will significantly impact your socialising experience.

2016 - With flatmates in Sydney, Australia.

If you choose to live on the outskirts of the city, you might find a home within your budget, often with the perk of having the entire flat to yourself. Alternatively, living closer to or within the city may require sharing accommodation with one or more people, but it comes with distinct advantages. You'll likely be closer to your workplace (or the university if you are a student), public transportation, and a wider social network.

Living outside the city may mean fewer resources and opportunities, as well as longer commutes. With fewer people around, your access to amenities and social connections could be limited. It's important to weigh these factors carefully when deciding where to live.

Socialising Rules - Important Rules to Follow When Making Friends

2024 - Interview with Arzu at Bollywood Boat Party in Sydney

Last year, I attended Sydney's renowned Bollywood party, where I had the chance to interview some desi girls about their experiences socialising in the city. They shared a few key tips for desi boys:

- **Be punctual** – Always arrive on time. Indians usually have a reputation for being late and keeping their friends waiting. This "Indian Standard Time" can be frustrating, especially for people from cultures where punctuality is a priority.

- **Smell good** – One party-goer I interviewed there mentioned that she wished *desis* would use good deodorant or perfume. She noted that many Indians often smelled of spices and curry or had noticeable body odour. Gentlemen and ladies- if you want to make a good impression and build connections, ensure you always smell fresh and pleasant.

- **Dance confidently** – Not everyone is a natural dancer, and that's okay. However, if you want to socialise and make friends, it's worth learning a few basic moves. If you're unsure, simply mirror your friends' steps and have fun!

In the next chapter, I have important dating-abroad tips for you!

Chapter 7

Dating and Relationships Abroad

Dating and finding love while living and working overseas as an Indian is a topic of considerable importance—one that is, unfortunately, often overlooked.

Many Indians who move abroad for work or studies are young, often of marriageable age, and frequently single. Naturally, the desire to build connections, find love, and explore the dating world is a common part of their experience.

However, the landscape of relationships has grown increasingly complex. Divorce rates are rising not only in India but also among Indians living abroad. In some cases, marriages are entered into for reasons such as obtaining citizenship or securing a visa, adding another layer of complexity to the dynamics of love and commitment. These factors have made modern dating a challenging journey.

This chapter addresses the realities of dating as an Indian abroad. I will provide practical tips, essential etiquette, and the unspoken rules of navigating the dating world in a foreign land. Additionally, I will also address the sensitive issue of the growing divorce rates among Indians and how these trends are shaping relationships.

Dreams Versus Marriage

Follow Your Dreams First: Love Will Find You

Have you seen the movie *Yeh Jawaani Hai Deewani?* It is my favourite! There's a brilliant scene where Ranbir Kapoor's character, Bunny, shares his dreams with Deepika Padukone's character, Naina. He shows her his vision book filled with photos of London, New York, and other incredible places, telling her he wants to visit every country.

2013 - Yeh Jawaani Hai Deewani - Bunny's Travel Dream Scene

Bunny also points out how life often feels like a predictable routine: we're students at 20, working by 25, parents by 30, and retired by 60. He's determined not to live such a dull, ordinary life—he dreams of doing something extraordinary, something big.

Back in our parents' day, life seemed simpler. You'd go to school, attend a decent university, get a stable job, get married, have kids, and retire. Job done. But our generation? We're wired differently. We want to chase our passions, see the world, and explore new opportunities—sometimes even moving overseas. For many of us, marriage isn't the first thing on the to-do list, and that's perfectly okay.

Waiting can be good for marriage. It gives you time to grow, figure out what you want, and build a stronger, happier relationship when the time comes. So, if you're not married yet, don't stress.

Here are some factors that people should consider first before they consider marriage:

Money Matters: Love, Life, and Responsibility

Let's face it—money plays a huge role in today's world. Like it or not, the moment your bank balance disappears (touch wood), there's a chance your love might waver too. Now, don't get me wrong—true love shouldn't be about money. But society? Oh, society loves to judge us by the numbers in our accounts. If you're flush with cash, you're suddenly seen as smart, wise, and oh-so-successful. Agree?

Here's another thing to think about: marriage brings extra responsibilities. Bills to pay, a home to manage, and maybe even kids to raise. If you don't have a solid financial base, how will you handle it all? That's why more and more people these days are waiting until their 30s to tie the knot—men and women alike.

It's not just about being practical; it's about giving yourself time to build a secure future. So, if you're focusing on your career and financial stability before marrying, you're not late to the party—you're setting the stage for a stronger, happier future.

Starting Life from Scratch

Another big reason many people are putting off marriage is the decision to move abroad. In India, life feels like a well-oiled machine—you've got your family home, perhaps a car, and a whole support network of friends and relatives. There's always someone to guide you, whether it's figuring out wedding plans or lending a hand with decisions.

But moving abroad? That's a whole new ball game. You're alone and most probably starting from scratch—finding a job, making friends, adapting to a different lifestyle, and saving up for essentials like a home and a car. Buying a house overseas isn't just expensive; it's a massive decision. Should you live close to work, settle in the city, or opt for the suburbs? Every choice takes time, energy, and a lot of planning.

In India, families often play a big role in weddings—parents, grandparents, and even extended relatives step in to help find the perfect partner, make arrangements, and guide you through decisions. But when you're abroad, it's all on you. With so much on your plate, it's no wonder that people prefer to take their time, settle in, and then think about marriage. It's a practical, thoughtful approach—and one that can make for a more stable, fulfilling life together.

Independence and the Challenges of Modern Relationships

Moving abroad makes you independent and more mature. You understand your worth and become pickier—you won't settle for less. In the past, options were limited, and a compromise was common. Now, with endless choices, swiping left to move on has become the norm for both men and women.

However, by your thirties, independence can make relationships tricky. When you marry young, you grow, change, and adjust with your partner. But when you marry in your thirties or forties, you've grown set in your ways, and change is harder to accept. If your partner dislikes something, you're more likely to say, "This is who I am."

When both sides are unwilling to adjust, it can lead to challenges, as relationships thrive on compromise.

That Brings Us Back to Dreams

Let me quote my favourite line from *Yeh Jawaani Hai Deewani*. Bunny's mother advises him. It is perfect for anyone thinking of giving up their dreams or settling down just for the sake of it.

"Live your dreams. Don't let pressure or questions from others weigh you down—everyone has their own battles to fight, and it's all about priorities."

Take your time to build a good life for yourself. Earn well, create a comfortable lifestyle, and truly enjoy life. Marriage can wait. In this incredible journey called marriage, happiness starts with you. Be content and complete on your own first—only then can you share that happiness with someone else. Remember, your joy doesn't come from another person. You are the one who completes you.

The Rising Indian Divorces - What's Going On?

Are divorces becoming more common among Indians, both within the country and abroad? Recently, the case of Bangalore tech professional Atul Subhash[3] made headlines. He left behind a 20-page suicide note detailing the harassment he faced from his wife.

References:

3. *Atul Subhash Suicide by NewsX Live*: https://youtu.be/8PKr6p0Ac7o

We were also surprised to hear rumours of Hardik Pandya and Natasa separating, especially after their affectionate posts on Instagram. It's even said that Natasa may have taken nearly 70% of Pandya's wealth. While he may recover financially, what about the emotional toll—his sense of family, love, and the impact on their child?

Imagine an Indian professional in his late 20s or early 30s, well-settled in London. He has a stable job, his visa is sorted, and he even holds a British passport. Now, he's ready to settle down and start a family. Wouldn't it make sense for him to find a partner already living in the UK? It would simplify many aspects—they can meet easily, there are no visa complications, and the prospective partner would already be familiar with the lifestyle.

Yet, many Indian men choose to return to India to find a spouse. This makes me wonder—why? Is it because they haven't adapted to the dating culture of their new country? Or perhaps they've been so focused on establishing themselves—finding accommodation, buying a car, and building a new life from scratch—that they haven't had time to explore relationships?

These men often return to India because they know they hold a higher status as NRIs (Non-Resident Indians). However, this can sometimes lead to complications. What if their prospective partner is primarily interested in securing a visa or citizenship? Worse still, what if that person struggles to adapt to life in London or wherever the NRI is based?

Here are four potential scenarios that might arise. While these situations don't occur every time, I'm sure you've come across such cases at some point.

Scenario 1: It's All About the Visa

The woman moves to London with her spouse and adapts effortlessly to the lifestyle. She upgrades herself, embracing new opportunities and experiences. Meanwhile, her husband remains unchanged, stuck in his ways. Over time, she realises there are far better-suited partners for her in London than her spouse. This scenario can just as easily apply to the opposite gender as well.

Scenario 2: The Wife Struggles to Adjust to Life Abroad

The woman finds it difficult to cope with the fast-paced lifestyle and cultural differences of a foreign country. She misses her family and the familiarity of life in India. Her husband, however, expects her to adapt quickly, encouraging her to embrace the lifestyle—wear modern clothes, accompany him to dinners, and present herself as his "arm candy" at social events.

Inevitably, comparisons arise with local women, putting additional pressure on her. Unfortunately, in many such cases, the frustration leads to the husbands mistreating their wives, sometimes even resorting to domestic abuse.

Scenario 3: Frauds and Scams

An NRI travels to India, gets married, and then returns abroad, leaving their spouse behind while their visa process is underway. The partner in India waits patiently, hoping to join them soon. However, the person abroad simply cuts off contact and disappears, leaving their spouse in a state of uncertainty and despair, often searching in vain for answers.

Scenario 4: Domestic Violence and Abuse

The couple begins living abroad, but differences soon emerge as they barely know each other. In a heated moment, the husband physically abuses the wife, prompting her to file an Apprehended Violence Order (AVO)[4]. This is in Australia; in the US it could be a restraining order. Such a legal order prevents the abuser from coming within 2 km/few miles of their spouse. Any breach of this order could result in imprisonment.

Such incidents are not uncommon—we often hear about them or read similar cases in the news. In some situations, the husband is exploiting the wife, while in others, it may be the reverse. I'm not trying to alarm or discourage you, but simply encouraging a pragmatic approach to such matters.

In the next section, I will share expert dating tips and insights that every single individual should know. From navigating visa basics to the art of being honest, we cover it all.

References:

4. Apprehended Violence Order:

https://www.police.nsw.gov.au/crime/domestic_and_family_violence/apprehended_violence_orders_avo

Important Dating Tips - Dos and Don'ts

Visa Status

This is super important! When you're dating someone, make sure you know what type of visa they're on—temporary, permanent, or resident. It's a big deal because dating abroad is very different from dating in India. Asking about their visa status isn't nosy; it's smart. These days, there are plenty of frauds and scams out there, and someone might just be looking for a spousal visa. So, do your homework and check their visa!

Be Honest About Your Own Visa Status

Whether you're on a student visa, permanent visa, work visa, or any other type, be upfront about it. Share where you live, what you do, and your relationship status—whether you're single, married, separated, divorced, or even married before.

These details matter a lot these days because no one wants to get caught up in legal troubles or accusations of dishonesty. Hiding the truth—or having the other person hide things from you—can lead to messy and unpleasant situations later on. Honesty from the start saves everyone a lot of trouble!

Grooming Tips

(Okay, since I am a guy, these tips may be more applicable to men. But I am sure women will also follow the same.)

Dress smartly whenever you go on a date. Choose a nice, crisp shirt or t-shirt, and avoid baggy or loose-fitting clothes—they're not in style anymore. If you have a beard, keep it neatly trimmed, and make sure your hair is well-groomed. Smelling good is essential, so don't skip on a bit of cologne or deodorant.

And here's a key tip—pay attention to your footwear! A good pair of shoes can make a big difference. These are simple yet important things every Indian living abroad should keep in mind. First impressions count!

Avoid Politics and Religion on the First Date

Steer clear of discussing politics or religion on your first date—it's a strict no-no. The other person may have different beliefs, follow a different religion, or support opposing political views. These topics are highly personal and can easily spark debates, arguments, or even outright disagreements.

Instead, keep the conversation casual and light. Focus on getting to know each other without diving into sensitive or divisive subjects. It's all about creating a comfortable and enjoyable atmosphere for both of you.

Keep the First Date Light and Short

When I go on a date, I like to keep the first one relaxed and short—something like a coffee or a light meal. If you both click, you can plan a more elaborate second date. But avoid long drives or fancy dinners right away. If you don't connect or things feel off, those long hours in a car or at an expensive restaurant can quickly become uncomfortable.

The key is to keep it short, sweet, and casual to start with. It's a much better way to get to know each other without any pressure.

Who Pays the Bill?

These days, most young people are earning, so both men and women can generally pay for themselves. However, I believe in being respectful. As a man, I usually insist on paying for the first date—it's a nice gesture, and many women appreciate it.

On future dates, pay attention to how the situation unfolds. If the woman suggests splitting the bill or offers to pay, take note. While it's important to be considerate, it's also fair to recognise that, over time, the expectation shouldn't always be for the man to cover the cost. We're all independent, so it's only right that a woman also contributes when appropriate. It's all about balance and mutual respect.

Don't Go in with Expectations

I have a simple philosophy when it comes to dating: You're spending one or two hours with someone who's also taking time out of their busy schedule. So, make the most of it—have fun, enjoy the conversation, and keep things light. But avoid diving into heavy topics like kids or finances. After the date, go your separate ways and reflect on how you felt. Did you like them? Do you want to pursue things further?

Go in with an open mind; without any fixed expectations. Expectations can lead to disappointments. If you feel like there's no connection, be respectful and honest. Let them know it's not working out and that you don't think you should continue dating. Thank them for their time and genuinely express your appreciation. It's all about keeping things kind and straightforward.

Respect Their Space and Behave Properly

If you ask someone out and they say they're busy, don't press them for details about what they're doing or where they're going. Respect their space. Similarly, if they're texting or taking a call while you're together, don't ask who they're texting or calling. Never snoop at someone's phone. If they want you to know, they'll tell you. This is especially important during the early stages of dating. Once you've been together for a while, you can ask or, even better, allow them to share willingly. Just make sure they feel like they have their breathing space.

Also, when you're with them, behave properly—look them in the eye while speaking. Don't look down, don't stare at their chest or behind, and definitely don't keep checking your phone. Girls notice where you look, guys—so please, be respectful. They pick up on your confidence, intentions, and gaze. They notice everything.

Don't Just Talk About Yourself
Make sure the conversation is a two-way street. Ask the other person about themselves—don't just focus on your own stories. Constantly talking about yourself can be a major turn-off for both men and women. Show respect by taking an interest in what they have to say. Ask about their hobbies, interests, work, likes, dislikes, and anything else that helps you get to know them better. It's about creating a balanced, engaging conversation.

Don't Bring Up S*x on the First Date

Avoid bringing up anything related to s*x or physical intimacy on the first date. Show courtesy and respect by not coming across as overly eager or desperate. Pay attention to their mood—if they bring it up and you feel comfortable, you can proceed. Generally, it's better to wait until the second or third date, again gauging the other person's comfort level.

I hope these tips on dos and don'ts help you navigate the dating scene abroad.

In the next chapter, I'll cover some important gym etiquette to help you maintain good physical health.

Chapter 8

Fitness Tips and Gym Etiquette Abroad

Your Health is Your Greatest Asset.

In today's world, nothing is more valuable than your health. As the saying goes, *"You'll forget 99% of your problems—until that 1% health issue shows up."*

Yet, when we move to a new country, health often takes a backseat. Long working hours, skipped workouts, and fast food become the routine for most of us. But neglecting your fitness and health will cost you far more later—in time, money, and well-being. Often, Indians abroad start taking their health seriously only after their doctor tells them to. But please remember- medical care can be very expensive overseas.

Staying active isn't just about physical strength; it also boosts mental health, reduces stress, and enhances overall happiness. This is why health and fitness are extremely important.

This also implies that gym culture has become a vital part of our lives. Gyms offer various options like weight training, cardio, yoga, and Pilates. But with this growing trend, gym etiquette is just as important.

In this chapter, I talk about the importance of health and fitness, supplements, staying fit despite a busy lifestyle, and how to embrace gym culture abroad while respecting others.

Your health is the foundation of everything—prioritise it, and the rest will follow.

You Can Be Fit and Build Muscle Even in Your 30s and 40s

Here are important tips to maintain muscles and fitness while enjoying good food

Diet, Fitness, Alcohol

I'm sure many of you enjoy drinking, and in some circles, social drinking plays a role in climbing the corporate ladder. However, I urge you to consider these three elements together—diet, alcohol, and fitness. Striking the right balance between them is crucial.

Sample Scenario:

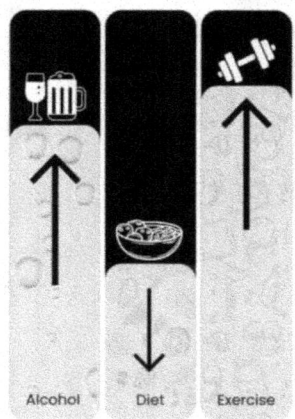

Drink more? Eat less and exercise more to balance it.

Drink less? Maintain a balanced diet and stay active.

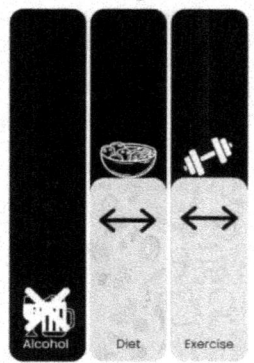

No alcohol? Focus on good nutrition and regular exercise.

What does this mean?

- If you drink alcohol regularly or heavily, you need to compensate by increasing your fitness levels while maintaining a healthy diet.

- If you don't drink alcohol, that's fantastic—it's one of the best things you can do for your body. In this case, your primary focus should be balancing your calorie intake (from your diet) with your calorie expenditure (through exercise), which I'll discuss shortly.

- If you neither drink alcohol nor exercise, you still need to pay close attention to your diet. Prioritise good nutrition—a healthy, balanced diet with the right proportions of protein, complex carbohydrates, fibre, and plenty of water. This approach will help prevent weight gain. That said, I firmly believe exercise is vital. Beyond physical benefits, exercise has profound effects on mental health and overall well-being. Most importantly, it supports a healthy metabolism, which brings me to my next point.

Metabolism

Metabolism is the engine of your body—it determines how efficiently you burn the calories you consume. Some people have a slower metabolism, while others have a faster or more efficient one. It's important never to compare yourself to others in this regard.

Some people seem to burn off whatever they eat with ease—whether it's alcohol or indulgent treats like ice cream—and never seem to gain weight. Meanwhile, others may struggle to burn calories effectively, gaining weight even when carefully watching their diet.

Calories Intake and Calories Burnt

Sample Scenario:

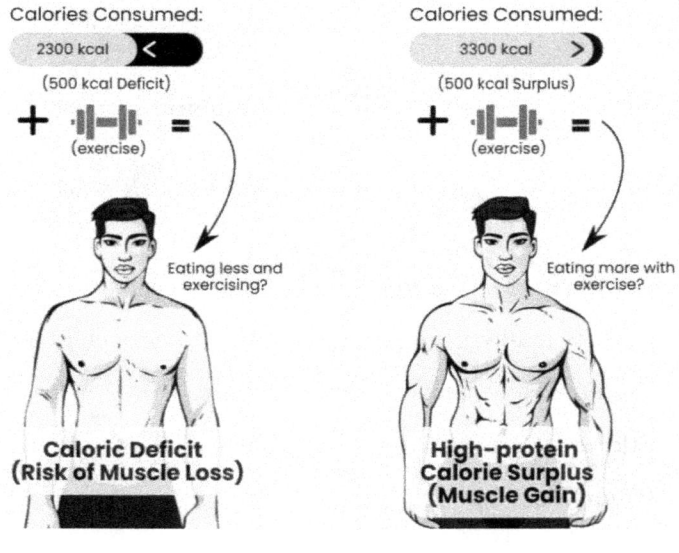

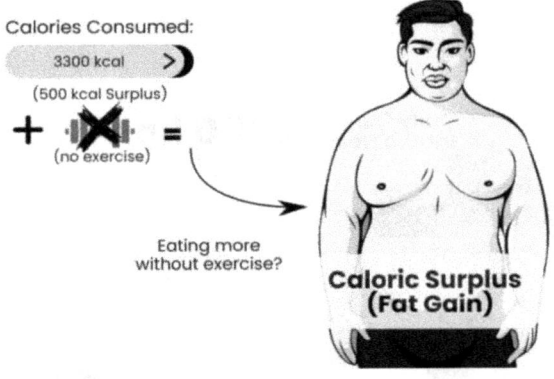

It's a simple formula: if you're overweight, burn more calories than you consume. If you're underweight and want to gain weight, consume more calories than you burn. Your calorie intake and expenditure should align with your BMI (Body Mass Index).

For example, based on my BMI and age, my recommended daily calorie intake is 2,800. If I consume fewer calories than this, I risk losing muscle mass. If I exceed this amount, I'll gain weight. However, by exercising and incorporating weightlifting while maintaining the right calorie intake, I can effectively burn fat and build muscle simultaneously.

Diet Control - Cheat Codes

You might ask me: Paras, I am unable to control myself. I am a foodie and I cannot stop eating my favourite foods. After all, what is life without good food? Okay, for such people, I have two cheat codes for you:

- **Cheat Code 1**

    If you struggle to control your portions or resist indulging in your favourite foods, the solution is simple: move more and exercise more. As long as you burn more calories than you consume, you can maintain a balance and need not worry about weight gain.

- **Cheat code 2**

    Try to eat slowly and mindfully. I often notice people rushing through their meals, especially when enjoying their favourite foods. Take your time, savour each bite, and allow your brain to register what you're eating. It takes approximately 15–20 minutes for your brain to recognise that your stomach is full. Eating slowly and mindfully not only aids digestion but also helps prevent overeating.

Tips for Maintaining Long-Term Fitness

Supplements - To Take or Not to Take?

The key word here is "supplement," meaning the protein supplements you take should complement your diet rather than replace it. If your dietary foundation is inadequate, simply taking supplements will not contribute to muscle building. The priority is to maintain a balanced, nutritious diet, engage in regular exercise, and ensure sufficient sleep. Only then will supplements effectively support your efforts.

Sample Scenario

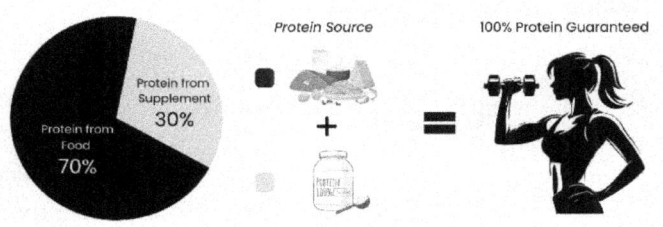

Food provides most of your protein needs and essential nutrients, while supplements help fill the gap to reach your daily goal.

Always remember: get your staple diet in order first. Only then will supplements truly be beneficial.

Motivational Fitness Tips for Busy Individuals

I often see many *desis* who move abroad, focusing solely on earning money and building a comfortable, beautiful life, while their health takes a backseat. This is especially concerning, as most migrate in their late 20s or 30s—a crucial period for prioritising health and well-being.

So, how do you stay motivated to look after yourself?

Mindset Matters

Mindset is incredibly important. If your focus is solely on making money, let me remind you: your health is your wealth. Without good health, you won't be able to fully enjoy the wealth you work so hard to create.

Let me illustrate this with an example. Imagine you're driving from Sydney to Melbourne, but you've filled your car with the wrong kind of fuel. No matter how much you push, the car will eventually break down. Your car needs the right fuel, regular tune-ups, and servicing to function properly. Now, think of your body as your "vehicle" for life. How can you expect it to last if you neglect proper nutrition and regular exercise?

This is the mindset you need to develop. Your body is the most important vehicle in your life. As Indians, we take great care of our cars—servicing them on time and fixing any issues promptly. So, why not show the same care and love to your body? A shift in mindset like this can inspire you to eat better, stay active, and prioritise your health.

What Type of Exercise is Best Suited for You?

Seek The Help of a Professional Trainer

I strongly recommend that you consult a qualified doctor or certified personal trainer to receive personalised advice tailored to your unique needs and health status. Before starting any form of physical activity, ensure you are medically fit and physically prepared to undertake it.

Start Slow

Begin at a pace that feels comfortable and gradually increase the intensity or duration as your fitness improves. Always listen to your body's signals and avoid overexertion, particularly in the early stages. Even moderate activities, such as a 30-minute walk, dancing, swimming, or similar exercises, are excellent starting points for beginners. These activities can help improve stamina and cardiovascular health without placing undue stress on your body.

Weight and Strength Training

As your body gets used to working out, start incorporating strength and weight training into your routine. Exercises involving weights, resistance, or bodyweight training are particularly important for maintaining and building muscle mass, which naturally declines with age. They also enhance bone density and overall strength, reducing the risk of injuries and supporting long-term mobility.

Additionally, practices like Pilates and yoga offer significant benefits by improving flexibility, balance, and core strength, while also promoting relaxation and mental well-being. These activities complement other forms of exercise, creating a balanced and holistic fitness routine.

Be Consistent

No matter what exercise you choose, the key to lasting success is consistency and patience. Set realistic goals, enjoy the journey, and take pride in the process of improving both your physical and mental well-being.

Injuries in the 30s and 40s And Tips to Avoid Them

Your 30s and 40s are often some of the busiest years of life. Between working hard, earning a living, and perhaps starting a family, fitness can easily take a back seat.

During this time, many of us spend long hours sitting, often slouching, which negatively affects our posture. This can lead to common issues such as neck pain, lower back pain, and knee discomfort. These problems are often the result of excessive computer use and a sedentary lifestyle. In fact, 95% of people[5] will experience lower back pain at least once in their lifetime.

As children, we were naturally active, but this often declines during university and even more so in professional life, where prolonged sitting becomes the norm. Spending hours in this position compresses the back muscles and takes a toll on the body over time.

References:
5. Global, regional, and national burden of low back pain, 1990–2020, its attributable risk factors, and projections to 2050: a systematic analysis of the Global Burden of Disease Study 2021: https://pmc.ncbi.nlm.nih.gov/articles/PMC10234592/

Get A Solid Foundation

When a stiff, poorly conditioned body is taken to the gym and asked to perform exercises like squats or deadlifts, it becomes highly susceptible to injuries. Without a proper foundation, the body struggles to perform at its best. The issue lies in the lack of preparation—many people fail to "prep" their bodies for exercise. Think of it like starting a car that hasn't been used in months; it takes time and effort to get it going smoothly.

Skipping warm-ups and stretches is a common mistake, but this oversight lays the groundwork for potential injuries. A tight, unprepared body will not respond well to physical exertion. Stretching and warming up are crucial steps in preparing your muscles and joints for exercise and reducing the risk of harm.

Aim to Move More

In addition to structured exercise, make an effort to incorporate more movement into your daily routine. For instance, walk while talking on the phone or during online meetings. Some workplaces now offer innovative solutions such as desks with attached cycles or treadmill desks, allowing people to move while working. Standing desks are also increasingly popular.

The key takeaway is simple: move more, and move often. Your body will thank you.

Seek Professional Guidance

To prevent injuries and optimise your fitness journey, seek professional guidance. A qualified personal trainer can assess your current fitness level and range of motion, identify weaknesses, and recommend exercises that are both safe and effective for your body. They can also help you progress at a pace that suits you, ensuring you avoid overexertion.

Gym Etiquette - Dos and Don'ts

Now I come to the most important part of this chapter. Rules to follow when you are in the gym.

Always Carry a Towel

We Indians, in particular, should follow this rule diligently. Our tropical skin tends to have larger pores, which means we sweat more than people of other nationalities. To maintain hygiene, always carry a towel to wipe off your sweat and ensure you cover any equipment, such as benches, before using them. This small habit goes a long way in keeping both yourself and others comfortable.

Don't Stare

Avoid staring at other gym-goers, whether men or women. Sometimes, this happens unintentionally—we may simply be admiring their workout or technique—but it can make people feel uncomfortable and is considered rude. For instance, men might look at women working out in the mirror, assuming they won't notice, but trust me, they can. If you admire someone, it's better to offer them a compliment rather than staring. Being respectful of others' space and privacy creates a more comfortable environment for everyone.

Don't Get Too Close to Someone When Working Out
This is an unspoken rule in many places overseas: no one stands too close to others, whether it's on the bus, at work, or especially in the gym. It's considered rude and can make the other person feel uncomfortable.

Additionally, there's a safety aspect to consider. If you or someone else is working out with dumbbells, being too close can result in serious injury. Of course, there may be times when the gym is crowded. In such situations, do your best to maintain personal space. Make eye contact and politely ask if it's alright to work out in that area. Always be mindful and cautious.

Put The Equipment Back in The Same Place

Most gyms, including those in India, have signs asking members to re-rack used weights and plates. It's important to remember that it's unfair to expect someone else to lift the 40-50 kg weights or plates you have used and put them away. Be courteous and always return the equipment to its proper place after use. This simple act of consideration helps maintain a safe, organised, and respectful environment for everyone.

Do Not Disturb Other People with Chit Chat

For many, the gym is a sacred space—much like a temple or a meditation centre. Avoid engaging in small talk, especially with those deeply focused on their workout or wearing earphones or headphones. Refrain from tapping them on the shoulder repeatedly, as this can be highly irritating. Only interrupt if it's absolutely necessary or genuinely important.

Use a Spotter or Hire a Professional Trainer

In Indian gyms, you can ask a fellow gym-goer to spot for you, or there are professional spotters available. However, overseas, it is highly recommended to hire professional trainers who can provide proper guidance, especially if you're new to working out.

This is crucial to help you prevent injuries and ensure you're using the correct techniques. While gym trainers may seem expensive and typically charge hourly rates, think of it as a valuable investment in your fitness journey. The benefits far outweigh the cost, and you'll be glad you made the choice.

Wear Proper Attire and Footwear

Avoid wearing inappropriate clothing, such as jeans or formal shoes, to the gym. Not only can this be uncomfortable, but it may also put your safety at risk. Instead, opt for proper dry-fit gym wear, which is widely available in most stores. It's designed to keep you comfortable, safe, and ready to perform at your best.

I hope these tips inspire you to embrace a fit and healthy lifestyle and empower you to truly thrive while working abroad.

Epilogue

A Story of Growth

I would like to leave you with a short story. Two young men were living in Delhi, both of whom secured admission to a prestigious New York University. Both had excellent marks and were preparing for their move to New York the following month. They were busy packing.

One of them, let's call him Aman, was practical and serious, aware of what he wanted and hardworking. Aman was from a lower-middle-class background.

Kabir   *Aman*

The other boy, Kabir, came from wealth, was pampered, and had no real experience of life. He was impractical and had everything handed to him, having led a sheltered existence. Both were preparing to start their new life abroad and began to think about accommodation in New York.

Kabir asked Aman, *"Why bother finding your own accommodation?* We can just stay in the university dorms." But Aman responded, *"Yes, the dorm is an option, but I know how things work. They will probably pair us with other Indian or Asian students. I have different goals, and I am thinking long-term."*

Kabir, confused, asked, *"What else do you need to study? The university will teach us everything."*

Aman replied, *"No, I'm talking about learning skills beyond what's taught in textbooks. I want to understand different cultures and interact with people from various nationalities. That's an important part of personal growth. This too is a form of learning."*

Kabir shrugged, *"Okay, you do whatever you want. I'm all set with the dorm. I've already paid for it as part of my fees."*

So, they both set off for New York. They said their goodbyes, and Kabir went to his dorm where he was surrounded by fellow students from India. Aman, on the other hand, chose to live in a flat with flatmates from different countries—Argentina, Germany, Brazil, Canada, and more.

On weekends, Kabir spent his time with his desi friends—attending Bollywood parties, speaking in Hindi, listening to Bollywood songs, and eating traditional Indian food. Meanwhile, Aman spent his weekends struggling to speak English and trying to get along with his flatmates. His flatmates cooked different cuisines, names of which he struggled to pronounce.

But he adapted. Of course, there were times he doubted whether he had made the right decision. He felt alone at times, missing his family, his friends, and Indian food. But he kept pushing through, learning and growing.

Slowly but surely, Aman began to adapt. He learned to cook, became friends with his flatmates, dressed well as they did, embraced their cultures, joined them at the gym, and worked on himself. He grew, learned important soft skills, and became more polished.

Meanwhile, Kabir continued to indulge in heavy drinking, never bothered to improve his English, and spent all his time with other Indian students. He never adapted to the new environment, gained weight from overeating Indian food, avoided exercise, and even took up smoking, living in dirty conditions.

One evening Kabir and some of his friends went to a pub. They drank heavily, and as was often the case, Kabir misbehaved, trying to hit on a girl. Aman happened to come there and asked the girl-. *"Is this guy bothering you?"*. She replied, *"Yes, he's been misbehaving with me."*

Aman, shocked by the sight of Kabir—dressed poorly, drunk, and acting inappropriately—turned to the girl and said, *"This is my friend Kabir. I'm sorry for his behaviour."* He turned to Kabir and said- *"Dude, this is my girlfriend!"* Aman's friends, a mix of people from all over the world, gathered around, offering their support. *"Are you okay, Aman?"* they asked. *"Is this guy bothering you?"*

Kabir, standing there, realised something: Aman had changed. He was polished, well-spoken, and surrounded by a sophisticated group of friends from diverse backgrounds. Aman's friends were classy and supportive, and Aman himself spoke to his girlfriend and friends in flawless English.

Kabir, looking at the situation, saw how much Aman had grown. He - Aman- had struggled in the beginning, but he had embraced new experiences, adapted, and flourished. He was now a different person—refined and accomplished. On the other hand, Kabir had stayed the same, comfortably nestled in his familiar circle, surrounded only by Indian friends, never stepping outside of his comfort zone.

Aman looked at his friend and asked, *"What have you done to yourself? How did you end up like this—drunk and unable to even hold a proper conversation?"* He glanced at Kabir's friends. *"Is this your circle now?"*

Kabir realised the painful truth: he had stayed in his comfort zone, never pushing himself to grow, while Aman had struggled in the beginning, but learned, and reaped the rewards. The difference between them was clear—Aman had adapted and thrived, while Kabir had stagnated.

Kabir vs. Aman

Tell me: which guy do you want to be?

Conclusion

8 Lessons for a Successful Life Abroad for NRIs

Living and working abroad is not easy—it requires significant adjustments and a willingness to adapt to a new environment. This book has been crafted to help you navigate these challenges and find success both personally and professionally.

One of the key aspects of thriving abroad is understanding and practising proper etiquette in public places. Whether it's queuing patiently, keeping noise levels low, or respecting personal space, these small acts demonstrate cultural sensitivity and create a positive impression. Similarly, office etiquette plays a vital role in professional success. Punctuality, effective communication, and good manners can help you build trust and credibility with colleagues and supervisors.

Socialising and making friends are another essential step in settling into a new country. Cultivating relationships requires effort—be proactive, attend social events, and express genuine interest in others. At the same time, keep an open mind about different cultures. Doing so not only broadens your perspective but also facilitates mutual respect.

Lastly, be mindful of your actions in public, such as keeping phone conversations discreet. This demonstrates awareness and respect for others around you. By incorporating these habits, you not only integrate seamlessly into your new environment but also **represent India with dignity and pride.**

ABOUT THE AUTHOR

Paras Kumar has spent the last 14 years living and working in countries like South Africa, the UK, and Australia. His journey of moving abroad came with its fair share of challenges like figuring out workplace culture, making new friends, and even dealing with difficult situations like racism. Through these experiences, he realised that while there's plenty of advice on visas and logistics, no one really talks about the everyday struggles of settling into a new country.

This inspired him to create Paras Perspective, a platform where he shares practical tips and real-life insights to help Indians feel more prepared and confident when moving overseas. Whether it's understanding workplace etiquette, navigating cultural differences, or building a social life, Paras provides relatable advice based on his own experiences. Over time, he has built a strong online community of Indians living abroad or planning to move, offering them the support and guidance he wished he had when he first moved.

While Paras Perspective has reached thousands through videos, Paras understands that not everyone prefers watching content online. Many people still enjoy reading in a classic, tangible format, and a book offers the advantage of having all the essential information in one place. This encouraged him to write Passport to Success, bringing together 8 important chapters making sure that his most valuable insights are available in a structured and comprehensive guide that readers can always turn to.

CONNECT WITH PARAS HERE:

🌐 Website: www.parasperspective.com
✉ Email: paras@parasperspective.com
📷 Instagram: @parasperspective
▶ YouTube